MEMORIES OF MIDDLESBROUGH
IN THE
1970S AND 1980S

TOSH WARWICK

This book is dedicated to the memory of my Mam, Kathleen Warwick, who passed away in June 2020. Many of the places featured in the book bring back memories of our regular trips to Middlesbrough that I will forever miss.

First Edition 2020
Published by Heritage Unlocked
www.heritageunlocked.com

British Library Cataloguing-in-Publication data
A catalogue record for this book is available
from the British Library

ISBN 9781913375157

Cover Photo: Teesside Archives
Book Design: Peter Hinton Design

CONTENTS

Introduction

The story of Middlesbrough as a town dates back less than two centuries to the emergence of the modern urban centre as a product of Victorian industrialisation and rapid urbanisation. Despite this relatively short urban history, the fascination and pride in Middlesbrough's heritage and history is very strong. It evokes poignant recollections and prompts lively debate, not least on the vibrant social media pages that boast tens of thousands of members and have provided an accessible, engaging way for more people to engage with Middlesbrough's heritage and history.

Numerous books explore historic Middlesbrough and the surrounding areas through old photographs from archives, libraries, museums and private collections. Many tend to focus heavily on Victorian and early twentieth century snaps of the town as an 'Ironopolis' and feature famous events, familiar buildings and postcard depictions of the area. *Memories of Middlesbrough in the 1970s and 1980s* includes many landmarks and themes explored in other publications but also explores places and subjects sometimes overlooked such as remnants of the industrial past, abandoned communities and the experience of everyday life in the town. Importantly, the book captures memories of those who experienced life in Middlesbrough during the seventies and eighties, a period that brought significant change for the town.

The iconic Royal Exchange was one of the historic buildings demolished in the 1980s to make way for the A66 (John Severs)

By focusing on this period, the book goes beyond the far removed high points of Edwardian civic culture and grandiose architectural triumphs and chronicles an area undergoing great transition and, in some instances, marked decline. The decades were a turbulent time for the communities along the Tees as industrial expansion in the 1970s was followed by 1980s recession, industrial strife and high unemployment. Middlesbrough Dock closed in 1980 and downstream at South Bank operations at Smith's Dock were drawing to a close by the mid-1980s. Although the Teesside Development Corporation threatened to rejuvenate the post-industrial landscape, there were few visible signs of progress in Middlesbrough by the end of our period. 'Progress' saw the development of new infrastructure coupled with the loss of historical buildings such as the Royal Exchange, built to serve the booming Ironopolis of the 1800s, to be replaced by the A66 that provided a transport artery to the communities and industries of Teesside. There were, of course, many cultural and social changes that occurred during the period too and some of these feature in this book, including the story of civic developments, Middlesbrough's music scene, new leisure and retail facilities and sporting glory.

The Transporter Bridge experienced a turbulent couple of decades (Teesside Archives)

The geographical coverage of this book goes beyond Middlesbrough as defined by municipal and parliamentary boundaries and includes Cargo Fleet, Grangetown and South Bank to the east of the town. Their inclusion reflects the fact many in these communities identify with and are culturally, economically and socially defined by their relationship with the former 'Ironopolis'.

I hope you enjoy this book and that it inspires you to dig out your old photographs and reminisce about Middlesbrough of yesteryear.

Dr Tosh Warwick, November 2020

Acknowledgements

I am grateful to John Severs for providing access to his collection of photographs and sharing his memories in this book. Thanks are due to Middlesbrough Libraries, Teesside Archives and *The Gazette* who have allowed reproduction of their material. Peter Hinton Design have also provided a fantastic service in designing this publication. *Memories of Middlesbrough in the 1970s and 1980s* features many memories and photographs shared by the local community and I hope the book reflects a range of recollections shared online in response to social media appeals. I would like to place on record my gratitude to historian Paul Stephenson (1944-2020) who shared his collection and his unique insights into Middlesbrough history with me. I wish to acknowledge the encouragement and support from those close to me, in particular Liberty who has been encouraging and displayed incredible patience throughout the process. Lastly, I would like to record my eternal gratitude to my late Mam for her support over the years and to whom *Memories of Middlesbrough in the 1970s and 1980s* is dedicated.

JOHN SEVERS COLLECTION: THE STORY BEHIND THE PHOTOGRAPHS

Memories of Middlesbrough in the 1970s and 1980s is inspired by John Severs' photography collection, which provides unique perspectives on Middlesbrough and the surrounding area during the 1970s and 1980s.

After leaving school, John started an engineering apprenticeship at ICI Billingham where he was surrounded by old plant that helped inspire his interest in industrial heritage. Around the age of 18, John's father, a wages clerk at Richie's Foundry and a keen photographer, bought the young engineer a camera and John started taking photographs of Cleveland ironstone mines and Middlesbrough's old buildings. John Severs' interest in old buildings and industrial sites is perhaps unsurprising given his family's strong connection to the former works and townscapes that feature in his photographs. His paternal great grandfather, Henry Severs, was a builder in Middlesbrough and his grandfather, William Severs, was a joiner at Teesside Bridge. John's maternal great grandfather worked in the blast furnaces at Cargo Fleet and his grandfather, Robert Shaw, was a riveter at Smith's Dock.

Teesside Bridge and Engineering Works on Cargo Fleet Road alongside the Middlesbrough to Saltburn railway line (John Severs)

As a legacy of this publication, many of John Severs' photographs have been deposited with Teesside Archives along with an oral history interview discussing the experience of capturing the area in the seventies and eighties. It is hoped that this will help inform and inspire future generations to explore Middlesbrough's history and the stories behind the photographs.

A PERIOD OF TRANSFORMATION

Teesside Councillors pictured in Middlesbrough Town Hall, 1970 (Teesside Archives)

The negative collections of Teesside Archives contain a number of photographs of councillors and council workers from the 1970s and provide an insight into the broader functions of the local government of the day. From 1968-1974, Middlesbrough was part of the County Borough of Teesside. The period brought a number of ambitious plans to enhance the area including through the Teesside Structure Plan that proposed an extensive overhaul of infrastructure, land use and transportation, as well as through enhancing the built environment by constructing new civic and commercial buildings.

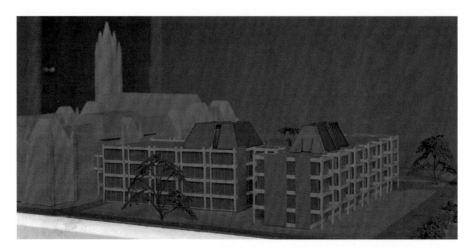

Model of the proposed new Civic Centre, 1970 (Teesside Archives)

One of the most notable developments of the period was the expansion of council offices around Middlesbrough Town Hall and Municipal Buildings, including the new Civic Centre that in 2020 is the home of a number of Middlesbrough Council departments.

Municipal buildings, Middlesbrough, 1970 (Teesside Archives)

The new buildings would provide an interesting contrast to the Victorian municipal buildings, to which they would be connected by a bridge.

Clearance work is carried out in preparation for the construction of the Civic Centre, 1971 (Teesside Archives)

The construction of the Civic Centre brought significant changes to the Middlesbrough townscape. This photo from 1971 shows demolition of premises around Middlesbrough Town Hall and Municipal Buildings to make way for the civic expansion.

Civic Centre construction work, November 1971 (Teesside Archives)

Council workers take a keen interest in the progress of the new Civic Centre as they look out from the windows of the Municipal Buildings in November 1971.

Middlesbrough Town Centre viewed from the Constantine Building, 1971 (Teesside Archives)

The changing townscape of Middlesbrough town centre was in evidence in the 1970s with the Cleveland Centre and Teesside Law Courts taking shape.

Cleveland Centre under construction, 1971 (Teesside Archives)

The Cleveland Centre takes shape in 1971 as Samuel Sadler looks on over Victoria Square. Note the statue's location in front of the Municipal Buildings before relocation in the early 2000s.

New Law Courts Foundation Stone (Teesside Archives)

The laying of the foundation stone ceremony for the new Law Courts, built on the site of Hugh Bell School, takes place on 23rd April 1971.

Progress at Victoria Square, May 1972. (Teesside Archives)

Progress continued in 1972 as the Middlesbrough skyline has a look more comparable to today with new civic and shopping complexes taking shape.

Victoria Square in 1980 (Teesside Archives)

People enjoy the sunshine in Victoria Square in 1980 with the changes to Middlesbrough's skyline evident in the background in the contrast between the new Corporation House and Middlesbrough Town Hall and Municipal Buildings.

Middlesbrough Central Library (Teesside Archives)

The gift of industrialist Andrew Carnegie and opened in 1912, the 1970s also brought changes for Middlesbrough Central Library in the form of extension work at the rear of the building.

An artist impression of the A66 published in the *Evening Gazette* in 1982 (Teesside Archives)

The decision to demolish the Royal Exchange in the early 1980s caused controversy and the *Evening Gazette* letters column featured a number of discussions on 'the dwindling number of relatively old or interesting buildings in Middlesbrough'.

Wilson Street, 1983 (Teesside Archives)

One of the most drastic changes of the 1980s was the transformation of the Wilson Street area. The construction of the A66 meant a number of buildings had to be demolished, although a number of buildings remained.

"I worked as a Tax Officer in Crown House in the early 1970s before moving to Teesdale House. Believing Crown House was going to be demolished for the A66, some staff on returning from Christmas lunch painted a frieze of Santa and his reindeers on the walls. After moving to Teesdale House it was revealed Crown House wouldn't be demolished and new staff would be moving in. I would love to have been a fly on the wall to see the reaction to the frieze!" - Kathleen Miles

The Brunswick (Teesside Archives)

The Brunswick Hotel public house was one such casualty of the new A66 Northern Route that cut through the historic heart of Middlesbrough.

Russell Street looking towards St John's Church (John Severs)

Beyond the A66 controversy, the 1970s and 1980s brought extensive clearance of housing and business properties with new residential and commercial premises taking their place. This photograph of Russell Street shows St John's Church and the Ironopolis Social Club before new housing and offices were built on the site.

Albert Road, 1970 (Teesside Archives)

George Guymer's fruit and vegetable shop and the Corporation Hotel are visible in this image of Albert Road in the 1970.

Corporation Hotel site, 1971 (Teesside Archives)

The birthplace of Wendy Richards of *EastEnders* Pauline Fowler fame, the Corporation Hotel was demolished to make way for Corporation House in the 1970s.

Famous Names and Familiar Places

Historic photographs provide an opportunity to look back and reminisce about famous names and familiar places that for many are still synonymous with the area even though the brands and buildings have disappeared. Some high street names are no longer in existence and their premises demolished. However, many of the buildings now have a new purpose and others retain their original purpose today.

Going shopping on Linthorpe Road, 1970 (Teesside Archives)

In the 1970s Linthorpe Road was home to a number of locally renowned names. These photographs from 1970 feature retailers including Pybus Bros., Sparks and Uptons.

Shoppers are captured on camera in 1979 near Camera Mart, 1979 (John Severs Collection)

Shoppers in 1979 pass Camera Mart with The Labour Club opposite and Tiffany's in the distance.

Forbes Buildings (John Severs)

Built initially as a bakery for John Forbes, the Forbes Buildings are awaiting a new roof in this photograph by John Severs.

Inside the Forbes Buildings, 1986 (Teesside Archives)

By the mid-1980s, the Forbes Buildings had diversified and included an art supplies shop, book centre and café.

Romer Parrish, 1971 (Teesside Archives)

For generations of children, Romer Parrish was a must-visit during any shopping trip. Pictured here in 1971, the store would continue to be the go to place for toys into the 1990s.

"I remember as a young boy travelling on the bus from Skelton to Middlesbrough and walking up to Romer Parrish's to spend my pocket money on the latest Subbuteo team. I remember proudly getting the iconic white band Boro side from there. It was probably Stuttgart's but it looked the same! Fantastic shop!" - Shaun Wilson

Constantine Building, early 1980s (Teesside Archives)

Opened in 1930 as Constantine College, the building has remained at the heart of Middlesbrough's higher education life throughout the decades as part of Teesside Polytechnic, University of Teesside and today's Teesside University.

Acklam Hall, 1973 (Glen Minford)

The Constantine Building and Teesside Polytechnic buildings were relatively new compared to other educational establishments in the town. These photographs capture the end of the school year for members of the Lower Sixth at Acklam High School, Acklam Hall and provide a great illustration of changing fashion!

Jack Hatfield's, Borough Road in 1973 (Paul Stephenson)

The sports store of Middlesbrough's Olympic Swimmer Jack Hatfield, the Borough Road shop was the place to go for football boots and kits for generations of Teessiders.

 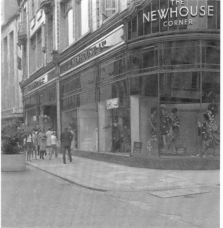

Newhouse's Corner, 1971 (Teesside Archives)

Newhouse's Corner was one of the main pre-planned meeting places for shoppers in Middlesbrough in the days before mobile phones. These photographs from 1971 capture some of the fashions of the day on show in the shop window.

British Home Stores, 1971 (Teesside Archives)

The demise of the BHS brand brought nostalgia for many Middlesbrough shoppers who frequented the store, seen here in 1971, for everything from school uniforms to evening attire.

Shoppers outside Marks & Spencer, 1972 (Teesside Archives)

Lots of familiar local and national names are on show in this photo of Linthorpe Road with Marks & Spencer, The Masham and H. Samuel among the nearby establishments. Note what looks like a painful incident for a man with a young child in the centre of the photo!

Shopper and Child (Teesside Archives)

On the theme of shoppers and children, Graham Ibbeson's 'Shopper and Child' stood outside the Cleveland Centre from 1983 until removal in the 1990s. Tees Valley Arts research on the public artwork has revealed that the two figures were modelled on the artist's wife and son, who is depicted pointing at his grandfather.

A busy Linthorpe Road in 1980 (Teesside Archives)

Linthorpe Road throngs with shoppers at the junction of Linthorpe Road and Corporation Road.

Alan Fearnley (*The Gazette*)

Alan Fearnley Records was one of Middlesbrough's favourite record shops of the era. Here, owner Alan Fearnley is pictured outside the shop in May 1984.

A pavement artist gets in the Christmas spirit in the 1980s (John Severs)

The festive spirit is all around in this image of Linthorpe Road in the 1980s as a pavement artist draws Santa, the Salvation Army band plays and shoppers set out to buy Christmas gifts.

Newboulds, 1971 (Teesside Archives)

Newboulds butchers, seen here tempting Linthorpe Road shoppers in 1971, was a famous Teesside name that has only recently disappeared from the high street.

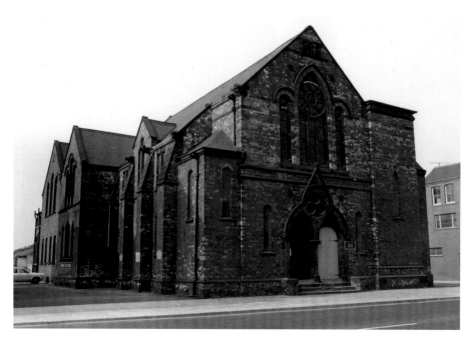

Cleveland Scientific Institute (Teesside Archives)

The Cleveland Scientific Institute was located on Corporation Road and played an important role in the industrial and scientific communities since industrialists converted the former Zion church into committee rooms, lecture and reception spaces and a library. The unlisted building's controversial demolition in 2006 led to widespread criticism of the contractors.

Marton Road, 1972 (Teesside Archives)

Bobby's Cycles catered for the biking needs of generations of Teessiders until its closure in 2017. Pictured here in 1972, The Borough Hotel (now Dr Brown's) is also visible on the extreme right of the image.

Telephone boxes outside Middlesbrough Town Hall, 1987 (Teesside Archives)

The row of telephone boxes outside Middlesbrough Town Hall, pictured in 1987, have become a familiar local landmark. The telephone boxes underwent refurbishment in 2020 in preparation for a new art installation.

North Riding Infirmary (Teesside Archives)

Opened in 1864 with a focus on providing emergency care for workers injured in the nearby Ironmasters' District, by the 1980s it was apparent that the Infirmary was on borrowed times with the opening of South Cleveland Hospital. The North Riding Infirmary closed in 2003 and was demolished in 2006 after an unsuccessful campaign to save the building.

GOING FOR A PINT

The Masham, 1974 (Teesside Archives)

A Middlesbrough institution and a rite of passage for many Teessiders, The Masham was one of the town's most notorious watering holes.

"Around 1977 The Masham was the first pub I tried to get served in and it was also the first pub to refuse to serve me! Never mind, I just popped into 'The Shaky' over the road for my virgin pint." - Stuart Thirkell

The Masham Hotel, 1987 (Teesside Archives)

Masham customers enjoy the outdoor seating in summer 1987. The pub's proximity to the town's shopping centre made it a popular destination for shoppers in the 1970s and 1980s. The building is now home to a sportswear and fashion shop.

The Shakespeare
(Teesside Archives)

Like the nearby Masham, The Shakespeare retains much of its tiled façade. Although now closed as a pub, the famous Bass Brewery's red triangle logo is still visible outside the building. Known locally as 'The Shaky', the building has functioned as an arcade and gym in recent times.

The Madison, 1988 (*The Gazette*)

Although a long time closed, the Madison still remains one of Middlesbrough's most talked about nightspots. This photo features contestants in the venue's Miss Madison competition of 1988.

"The first ever nightclub I went to was the Madison for the South Park 6th Form College Christmas party in 1980. While most of my mates tried to get fixed up, I spotted Craig Johnston, the amazing Australian Middlesbrough player and talked footy and Boro with him all evening. He was a really nice bloke and I always respected him for taking time out to speak to a total Boro obsessive." - Chris Bartley

Eileen Liggitt working behind the bar in the Madison, c.1980s (Eileen Liggitt)

Sharing old photographs of the Madison on social media has encouraged a number of people to share their memories and photographs of the Madison, including this from Eileen Liggitt via Memories of Middlesbrough showing her working behind the bar around the 1980s.

"I met my now wife in the Madison in 1980. I've been married 34 years and have two lovely children, Claire and James, and grandson Oliver. I am so grateful to the Madison...it changed my life!" - Billy Wilde.

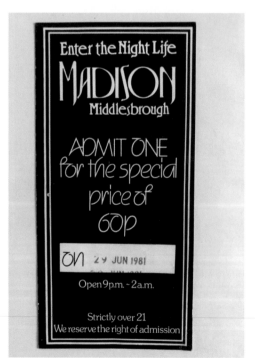

Enter the Night Life

MADISON
Middlesbrough

ADMIT ONE
for the special
price of
60p

ON 2 9 JUN 1981

Open 9 p.m. - 2 a.m.

Strictly over 21
We reserve the right of admission

Admit One - an admission ticket for the Madison (Billy Wilde)

The Wellington Hotel, c.1980s (Teesside Archives)

Once Middlesbrough's last men only pub, the former Wellington Hotel or "Welly" is now home to the Flares and Popworld nightclub and houses a boxing club upstairs.

"Every Friday and Saturday night we'd meet upstairs for a game of snooker then go downstairs for the music, which at times resembled a Wild West show!" - Harry Catterson

"I met my late wife there in April 1979, it was the place to be and the music at that time was absolutely amazing. Good times and lovely memories." - Gary Edward Mendum

The Albert, c.1980s (Teesside Archives)

The Albert pub, pictured in the 1980s, has been renovated in recent years as part of the Albert North regeneration project.

The Lord Raglan, Corporation Road (Teesside Archives)

At the very heart of Corporation Road, the Lord Raglan was once a thriving pub. When performing at nearby Middlesbrough Town Hall in 1972 it is said legendary rock star David Bowie visited the pub.

"My wife and I celebrated our engagement with dinner at the Lord Raglan on 4th May 1970. We had prawn cocktail followed by steak and chips - typical 1970s food. The manager then was Chisholm Spence. He introduced himself to us because of our name connection. He gave us a token as a small memento of the evening. We still have it somewhere safe but I can't find it at the moment!" - Malcolm Chisholm

The Empire, Linthorpe Road
(Teesside Archives)

The Empire pub on Linthorpe Road was a favourite of Boro fans as a stop off on the way to Ayresome Park. The venue has had numerous names in recent decades including The House, The Tavern and is now The Swatters Carr.

"I remember it well and always remember the banter with the away fans as the police marched them up Linthorpe Road from the station." - David Weaver

"Ahh ,The Empire! As a young kid I wondered what people were doing out the side door on my way to Fearnleys, then snuck in on my way to the match. It was my pub of choice as a young student going to gigs. I still call it The Empire." - Gordon Dalton

The Gosford Arms (John Severs)

Dating back to Victorian Middlesbrough, The Gosford Arms on Gosford Street is one of a number of pubs that have disappeared from St Hilda's or 'over the border'.
"All the pubs 'over the border' were class. The Gosford Arms was a brilliant pub. The landlord and local people were like one big family." - Steve Woodier

"Spent many a time in the Gosford with many great people. I played in the football, pool, dominoes and tug o' war teams. The coal fire in the winter months was unbeatable. A lot of unforgettable memories with a lot of great mates, most I still see today, in the best public bar any regular could ever ask for." - Arthur Hayes

The Fleece, South Street (John Severs)

Depopulation and declining industry in St Hilda's contributed to the closing and demolition of a number of pubs, including The Fleece.

The Ship Inn (John Severs)

The Ship Inn, licensed in 1831 and with it once Middlesbrough's oldest pub, is a recent casualty of the demolition of housing in St Hilda's and the loss of a local community to serve. Extensive fire damage has necessitated demolition of this historic watering hole in recent times.

Captain Cook (John Severs)

Dating back to the nineteenth century, the Captain Cook served locals and many visitors from around the world calling at Middlesbrough Dock. The pub featured in the *Auf Wiedersehen, Pet* series in which the Transporter Bridge was relocated to Arizona! In 2020, the Captain Cook was named on The Victorian Society's national Top 10 Most Endangered Buildings list.

The Albion, 1970s (John Severs)

Located on the corner of Dock Street and Lower Commercial Street, The Albion pub served the community around Middlesbrough Dock for over a century but by the 1980s found itself struggling amidst industrial decline. The building was demolished in the 1990s and today the site forms part of the Middlesbrough College complex at Middlehaven.

The Lord Byron, 1972 (John Served)

Few pubs survive in the area today although the Lord Byron on Bridge Street East has in the past decade reopened and serves the matchday crowds heading to the Riverside Stadium.

The Zetland (Teesside Archives)

One of Middlesbrough's architectural gems in the shadow of the Railway Station, The Zetland is Grade II Listed and boasts a stunning tiled back room that is of national heritage significance.

Inside the Zetland, mid 1980s (Teesside Archives)

These photographs from the 1980s capture the space before refurbishment works in the 2010s that saw the bar removed and the back room converted into Christie's Brasserie.

"My Mam and Dad ran The Zetland in the early eighties. I was about 14 - let's say my eyes were opened! I have fond memories of it. We used to get people coming in to take photos of the lounge and there was a secret room underneath which looked like it was used for gambling. On Christmas Day, Dad would give a free drink to the regulars." - Glenn Usher

The Rock Garden (*The Gazette*)

Once one of Middlesbrough's premier music venues, The Rock Garden attracted a range of household names over the years including The Clash, The Stranglers and The Sex Pistols (as Acne Rabble) in 1977.

The Clash perform at The Rock Garden, 1977 (*The Gazette*)

The appearance of Acne Rabble led to fans without tickets turning up at the venue which, according to the Evening Gazette, led to angry scenes and police dispersing the crowd. The venue later became The Arena nightclub but in November 2020 stood empty.

Ossies Bar (Teesside Archives)

Ossies Bar was one of Middlesbrough's leading music venues and attracted a number of famous bands over the years.
"I was one of 30 people that watched The Wedding Present there. I remember before the gig they were sitting at tables that were converted from old Singer sewing machines and they were all loving frantically pedalling away on the foot pedals." - Robert Nichols.

THE HISTORIC QUARTER

The Historic Quarter around Exchange Square and the Railway Station contains a number of nationally and locally listed buildings and was once the epicentre of Middlesbrough's commercial life.

During the 1970s and 1980s, the area underwent extensive changes owing to the construction of the A66, with many historic buildings demolished and others refurbished. In 2020, the area was designated Middlesbrough's Historic England High Street Heritage Action Zone as part of a scheme to regenerate historic buildings and public spaces.

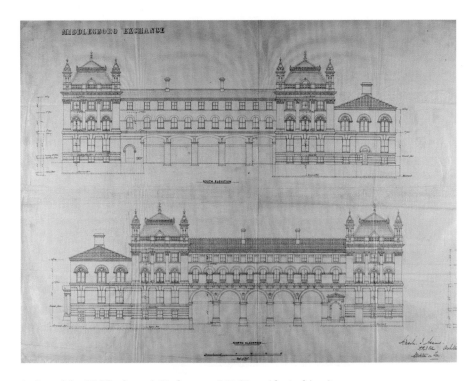

A plan of the Middlesbrough Exchange, 1866 (Teesside Archives)

The most striking building that disappeared from the Middlesbrough skyline as a result of the new road was the Royal Exchange. Designed by Charles John Adams, the Royal Exchange opened in 1868 initially as an iron and steel exchange for Middlesbrough's industries.

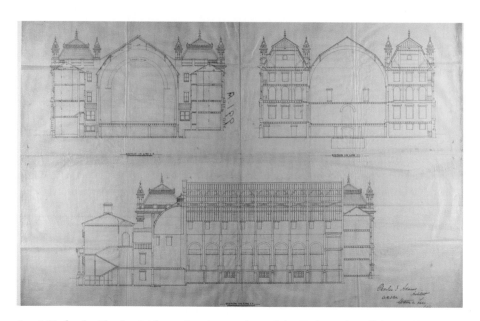

An 1866 plan by Charles J Adams showing sections of the Exchange's Hall (Teesside Archives)

During over a century of use, the grandiose building was home to a range of businesses and organisations including the offices of manufacturing firms, merchants and printers. It played host to the meetings of the Cleveland Club and was the host venue for a number of 'red letter day' events in the town's history, including the 1881 Middlesbrough Jubilee celebrations.

Drawing Office staff, Royal Exchange (Teesside Archives, British Steel Collection)

The building is best remembered as the former home of Dorman Long (later British Steel). These mid-century photographs of Dorman Long Drawing Office staff at work in the Royal Exchange provide a sense of the building's scale.

At work in the Royal Exchange (Teesside Archives, British Steel Collection)

The Drawing Office staff were packed in tight at the Royal Exchange in the 1950s as they produced plans for structures around the world and closer to home, including Dorman Long's Lackenby Works.

Looking south towards the Royal Exchange and Albert Road (John Severs)

In a 1981 survey of the town's historic buildings, the Royal Exchange was described as in 'fair' condition. Prior to demolition, the building had been empty since British Steel left the premises in 1977 and relocated operations to Steel House and other company sites.

"I started working for BSC in 1971 as a trainee. After a six week induction course at Redcar College I worked first in Zetland Road, Dock Street and then in the Office Manager's office in the Royal Exchange. Working there meant walking along the balcony that overlooked the draughtsmen below. My main job was booking transport for staff travelling to other BSC locations across the country. Going into work, I felt pride walking up the front steps of such an imposing building." - Joyce Duffie

Middlesbrough Town Hall in the distance with the Royal Exchange on the right (John Severs)

The 1981 report also noted that the building, possessing 'rich architectural detailing to the interior', was in the line of the A66 'Northern Route' which would likely require demolition of Adams' creation.

Exchange Hall, early 1980s (Teesside Archives)

A rare glimpse inside the grand Royal Exchange's Hall in the early 1980s.

Dorman Long, Royal Exchange (John Severs)

The name of world-famous Middlesbrough iron and steel firm Dorman Long was above the entrance to the Royal Exchange.

Grand Old Lady's Last Days (*The Gazette* & Teesside Archives)

In August 1984, the *Evening Gazette* reported on the last days of the Royal Exchange and revealed problems with dry rot, a leaking roof, structural issues and extensive vandalism.

GREAT HEART THAT HAS BEEN STILLED

Grand old lady's last days

ONCE it stood tall and proud, the pulsing heart of Teesside's booming iron and steel trade.

A thousand brokers milled below its barrel vaulted ceiling, a thousand deals were forged and struck in steel within its walls. Fortunes were made, fortunes lost.

Today, more than a century later, brash young Teesside's Klondyke-like business boom is well and truly over.

And the Royal Exchange, the grand old lady of Middlesbrough's commercial past, is on her last legs.

From the outside, time seems to have done little to wither the huge Victorian edifice that looms like the Kremlin at the end of Albert Road.

But on the inside, where only the ghosts of the Ironmasters tread, vandalism, dry rot and the ravages of

Story by CHRIS ELLIOTT
Picture by NIGEL LEONARD

the weather have taken their ugly toll.

The great revolving doors opening onto the central hall, with its domed pink and blue plastered ceiling, are rusted to a standstill.

A rabbit-warren of offices, once the nerve centre of enterprise, stand silent and empty.

Through their shattered windows, the sound of progress rushes in — the roar of town centre traffic in whose cause the 116-year-old Exchange will finally be razed to the ground.

The Exchange is being demolished to make way for Middlesbrough's new bypass, and the contractors will be moving in within the next few months.

It is expected demolition itself will take place about Christmas time.

Two of the men overseeing the bulldozers will be Cleveland's highways and bridges division chief assistant engineer Bill Douglas, and his deputy Alan MacDonald.

Said Alan: "It is an amazing building, and I'm sure a lot of people will be sad to see it go.

"The Exchange was once the hub of the business life of Teesside and beyond — world steel prices were fixed there, and it was as much a meeting place for the business community as anything else."

The grand old building was designed by Charles John Adams of Stockton, and work began in 1866. It took just two years to complete and the Exchange was open for business by July 28, 1868.

The first tenants were the Middlesbrough Exchange Co. Ltd. and the Cleveland Club, who traded there until just after the Second World War, when Dorman Long took them over.

Dorman Long converted the building into a massive suite of offices. It was there the enormous task of designing and processing the plans for the Lackenby steel plant and beam mill was carried out.

Until 1977, British Steel used the building for design work. Since the corporation pulled out, the building has been unused.

Only the Bodega bar, in the basement of the building, now remains.

The rest of the Exchange is an empty, glass-strewn shell. Vandals and tramps have wreaked widespread damage.

Said Alan: "Every effort has been made to keep the wreckers out, but it's an almost impossible task. They have caused considerable damage.

"As well as that, the building is riddled with dry rot, and the rain has been leaking through the roof."

For the workers who will eventually tear the building to the ground, it will be a painstakingly slow — and even hazardous — job.

Some of the building fabric contains asbestos, and the floors in some areas are so rotten they won't stand a man's weight.

The imminent destruction of the Royal Exchange has sparked several controversies.

Two years ago, campaigners battling to preserve the old building forced a public inquiry, but they lost their case.

In recent weeks, local councillors became embroiled in argument over suggestions that part of it might be saved.

It was thought the demolition men might rescue one of the building's four towers, or pavilions, but the idea was shelved when it emerged the cost of doing so could top £140,000.

● ALAN MacDonald, left, and Bill Douglas, in the shell of the Royal Exchange.

Bodega bows out

10.9.84

LAST orders for the Bodega bar.

Bodega Bows Out, 1984 (*The Gazette* & Teesside Archives)

The demolition meant the end for the Bodega bar and restaurant, a popular venue located downstairs in the Royal Exchange.

"END of an era" is a phrase that slips all too easily off the journalistic tongue, but in the case of the Bodega bar and restaurant in Middlesbrough, it is only too true.

After well over a hundred years in business, the downstairs haunt of generations of winers and diners in the Royal Exchange buildings will close its doors for the last time this week.

The end of the Bodega is more than just another closure; it's the severing of yet another link with Middlesbrough's all-too little past.

For around 120 years customers have tramped down the stairs to the single bar — with restaurant attached — while the traffic sped by at street level. When it opened horse-drawn vehicles clattered up Albert Road; now heavy lorries pound the growing wasteland which is to become the Northern Route.

The Bodega holds a special place in the affections of many. For years it was a men only bar and the bulk of its clientele are still professional gents from the offices which throng the commercial centre of Middlesbrough.

For this reason it enjoyed eccentric opening hours, mainly lunchtime and early evening and many are the trains missed because of lingering too long over a pint and a chat.

And for the Winterschladen family the closure of the Bodega is the breaking of a family link which goes back to those early days of the town.

The present manager, Robin Winterschladen, 26, is the fourth generation of the family to be connected with the business. His great-grandfather, who came from Germany, opened up as a wine merchant in the Royal Exchange in the 1860s. The dining room followed in 1880.

When the drinks business was sold to the supermarket chain Hintons, Robin's father, Jim reopened the Bodega on his own account.

Now the shutters are going up, last orders called and until the building comes down, only the ghosts of drinkers past will be left to inhabit the deserted Bodega bar.

David Hutchinson

Danger - Demolition in Progress at the Royal Exchange, 1984/85 (Teesside Archives)

A sign warns of danger as demolition of the former iron and steel exchange gets underway in the mid-1980s.

Demolition of the Royal Exchange, 1984/85 (Teesside Archives)

Despite concerns at the loss of the historic building, demolition went ahead in preparation for the construction of the new A66.

Rubble piles up at the Royal Exchange, 1984/85 (Teesside Archives)

Rubble piles up as the iconic Middlesbrough building disappears from the landscape.

Resurfacing work at Marton Road, 1902 (Teesside Archives)

This photograph captures resurfacing work around the Royal Exchange in 1902.

Resurfacing of Exchange Square, 1987 (Teesside Archives)

Here is the same area some 85 years on following the demolition of the Royal Exchange. There are some reminders of Charles John Adams' architectural masterpiece in Exchange Square today, including the relocated statue of ironmaster Henry Bolckow and a number of keystones from the Royal Exchange.

Jordison's, c.1980s (Teesside Archives)

Jordison's printers were a stone's throw from the Royal Exchange. The company was responsible for printing some of Middlesbrough's early newspapers and the Jordison name appears on numerous railway and wartime propaganda posters. Despite attempts to relocate part of the building to Peterborough as a museum, the A66 scheme saw the structure felled.

Masonic Hall (John Severs)

Masters Nightspot in the former Masonic Hall on Marton Road was one of a number of drinking establishments demolished in the 1980s owing to the construction of the A66.

The Post Office Buildings, 1978
(Teesside Archives)

Although the Royal Exchange is no
more, a number of historic
buildings survived the construction
of the A66 and play an important
part in cultural and economic life
today. The former Post Office
Buildings, adorned with a 'To Let'
sign in this late 1970s photograph,
later housed the county archives
service and is now home to
Teesside Archives.

Renovation of Middlesbrough
Railway Station's Main Booking
Hall, 1978 (Teesside Archives)

During the late 1970s,
Middlesbrough Railway Station's
Booking Hall underwent renovation.
The Winterschladen's Wine
Merchants and Tobacconists below
would later house the Cornerhouse
nightclub.

The Midland Bank (Teesside Archives)

The area around the Royal Exchange was once Middlesbrough's financial epicentre and included a number of banks. The former Midland Bank building with its distinctive copper dome is now part of the Commerce House serviced office and conference facility.

Lloyds Chambers, 1974 (Teesside Archives)

The Grade II Listed Lloyds Chambers, pictured here in 1974, is another of the area's commercial premises that has changed use several times. Initially built as a department store, since its use as a bank it has served as home to the Ayresome Park pub and most recently as a nightclub.

The Yorkshire Bank (Teesside Archives)

Designed by Gordon G. Hoskins, architect of Middlesbrough Town Hall, the former bank building once included residence for the bank manager. The premises is now Spensley's Emporium.

Zetland Buildings, 1980s (Teesside Archives)

Zetland Buildings, currently Grade II Listed, were home to a variety of businesses and clubs in the 1970s and 1980s including a British Railways Staff Association Club, Hank Sharpe Travel and Royal Liver Assurance.

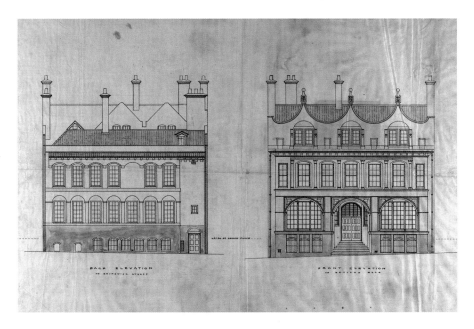

An 1889 plan of Webb House (Teesside Archives)

Despite the loss of a number of buildings at the heart of Middlesbrough's nineteenth century commercial centre, one of the most notable landmarks to remain is Webb House.

Webb House (John Severs)

Designed by celebrated Arts & Crafts architect Philip Webb, the Zetland Road building served as the headquarters of Bell Brothers and Dorman Long.

Cleveland Buildings, 1970 (Teesside Archives)

Workmen dig up the pavement around the Cleveland Buildings in 1970 with the Transporter Bridge visible in the distance. Formerly the homes of ironmasters Henry Bolckow and John Vaughan, the Cleveland Buildings are today known as Plenary BV House.

National Provincial Bank, c.1980s (Teesside Archives)

The former National Provincial Bank, pictured here around the 1980s, has undergone regeneration as part of the BOHO Zone in recent years, having previously been home to the Cleveland Club and a retail outlet.

Lost Communities: Cannon Street and St Hilda's

Few areas experienced change during the 1970s and 1980s more than the Cannon Street and St Hilda's or 'Over the Border' areas. The 1970s brought continued demolition of the Cannon Street area that had commenced in the previous decade, whilst the decline of industry around the Dock and River Tees meant many of the communities moved away from St Hilda's.

St Columba's Church, c.1970s (John Severs)

The landscape of the Cannon Street area has changed with the development of new commercial premises. Here John Severs photographs of St Columba's Church on the edge of the Cannon Street area reveal vast empty spaces left by demolition.

Marsh Road, viewed from the A66 embankment (John Severs)

Whilst the skyline of St Hilda's has changed in recent decades with the demolition of post-war housing, the Old Town Hall and Tees Transporter Bridge remain key historical features of the area.

St Patrick's RC Church (John Severs)

Serving the Catholics of Cannon Street, St Patrick's RC Church was at the heart of the community. Although almost all of the area was flattened by the late 1970s, the church remained standing and in use into the 1990s.

St Patrick's RC Church, 1986
(Teesside Archives)

The Friendship Club Writers'
Group's *Cannon Street: Lest
We Forget*, published in 1993,
described the church as
'isolated in its splendour in the
centre of the present industrial
estate'. On 11th October 2002,
a final mass was held before
the church was demolished.

Housing, St Hilda's (John Severs)

The new social housing built in St Hilda's in the 1950s and 1960s sought to provide
improved residential properties in the area. However, by the 1980s much of the housing
was dilapidated and even more recent housing was demolished in the 2010s.

The Old Town Hall viewed from Lower West Street (John Severs)

The Old Town Hall was once at the heart of Middlesbrough's St Hilda's Market Place. In this photograph by John Severs the landmark is flanked by modern housing.

The Old Town Hall, c.1980s (Teesside Archives)

The Old Town Hall served as a community centre, medical centre and library during the 1970s and 1980s but has since fallen into disrepair. Successive councils have drafted proposals to bring the building back in to use as part of Middlehaven regeneration schemes but each attempt has failed to bring any change.

Vulcan Street with the Transporter Bridge in the distance (John Severs)

The Vulcan Street Wall forms the boundary of the former Bolckow Vaughan ironworks and the Cleveland Salt Works and remains in place today.

Vulcan Street looking towards Middlesbrough Dock (John Severs)

A view looking along Vulcan Street towards the Middlesbrough Dock Clock, reputed to possess only three faces to prevent workers in the nearby industries clock-watching.

The Middlesbrough Dock Clock Tower, 1980 (Middlesbrough Libraries)

All quiet at Middlesbrough Dock Clock Tower as one man and his dog are dwarfed by the landmark, which contained water tanks and mechanisms that operated the dock gates.

Middlesbrough Dock, 1971 (Teesside Archives)

The cranes skirting Middlesbrough Dock are visible from Middlesbrough town centre in 1971, framed by today's Empire.

Middlesbrough Dock cranes dominate the skyline (John Severs)

The closure of Middlesbrough Dock in 1980 saw a number of the newer cranes transferred to Tees Dock. Regeneration around the area has occurred in recent decades and today Middlesbrough College along with the offices of *The Gazette* and Thirteen Group stand where cranes once stood.

A TV star in the Dock (John Severs)

The schooner Charlotte Rhodes of *The Onedin Line* TV fame visits Middlesbrough Dock in the 1970s as part of a tour which also included stops at various docks and ports throughout Britain.

HMS Devonshire visits Middlesbrough (John Severs)

The first of the Royal Navy's County Class guided missile destroyers, HMS Devonshire visits Middlesbrough Dock in 1976.

HMS Devonshire with Middlesbrough Dock Swing Bridge in the distance (John Severs)

Some 6,000 people went on board HMS Devonshire during the two open afternoons and 600 children from 15 schools enjoyed guided tours. Whilst in Middlesbrough members of the ship's company attended Ayresome Park to watch Boro's match against Ipswich Town and visited ICI, a Shell Refinery and local breweries.

THE STEEL RIVER

The seventies and eighties proved to be turbulent decades for the industries along the River Tees, famed as Chris Rea's 'Steel River'. Many of the iron, steel and shipbuilding industries disappeared from the riverside and those that remained faced the challenges of industrial decline.

Approaching Middlesbrough, 1977 (Teesside Archives)

The River Tees is visible on the left of Newport Marshalling Yard with the Tees Newport Bridge, Cannon Street gasholders and Transporter Bridge in the distance.

Tees Newport Bridge, 1972 (John Severs)

The decline of larger shipping traffic upstream at Stockton and Thornaby, most notably owing to the closure of Head Wrightson, meant the need to lift the Tees Newport Bridge diminished. Here the vertical lift bridge is raised in 1972 to allow the tugboat John H Amos to be towed to Stockton's Corporation Quay.

John H Amos, 1972 (John Severs)

The John H Amos moored at Corporation Quay, Stockton in 1972.

The John H Amos, renamed Hero, heads downstream as the tug starts a long journey to a new home at Chatham. The event attracted a great deal of interest and hundreds lined the banks of the 'Steel River'. The A19 Flyover is visible as the newest crossing of the River Tees.

Tees Newport Bridge (Paul Sherwood)

The Tees Newport Bridge is elevated with the last of the Cannon Street houses visible to the left and the remnants of Newport Ironworks to the right.

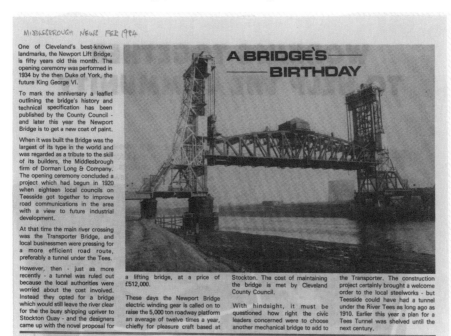

MIDDLESBROUGH NEWS FEB 1984

A BRIDGE'S BIRTHDAY

One of Cleveland's best-known landmarks, the Newport Lift Bridge, is fifty years old this month. The opening ceremony was performed in 1934 by the then Duke of York, the future King George VI.

To mark the anniversary a leaflet outlining the bridge's history and technical specification has been published by the County Council - and later this year the Newport Bridge is to get a new coat of paint.

When it was built the Bridge was the largest of its type in the world and was regarded as a tribute to the skill of its builders, the Middlesbrough firm of Dorman Long & Company. The opening ceremony concluded a project which had begun in 1920 when eighteen local councils on Teesside got together to improve road communications in the area with a view to future industrial development.

At that time the main river crossing was the Transporter Bridge, and local businessmen were pressing for a more efficient road route, preferably a tunnel under the Tees.

However, then - just as more recently - a tunnel was ruled out because the local authorities were worried about the cost involved. Instead they opted for a bridge which would still leave the river clear for the the busy shipping upriver to Stockton Quay - and the designers came up with the novel proposal for a lifting bridge, at a price of £512,000.

These days the Newport Bridge electric winding gear is called on to raise the 5,000 ton roadway platform an average of twelve times a year, chiefly for pleasure craft based at Stockton. The cost of maintaining the bridge is met by Cleveland County Council.

With hindsight, it must be questioned how right the civic leaders concerned were to choose another mechanical bridge to add to the Transporter. The construction project certainly brought a welcome order to the local steelworks - but Teesside could have had a tunnel under the River Tees as long ago as 1910. Earlier this year a plan for a Tees Tunnel was shelved until the next century.

A Bridge Birthday, 1984 (Middlesbrough News & Paul Stephenson)

Constructed by Dorman Long in 1934, the Tees Newport Bridge celebrated its 50th anniversary in 1984, by which time it was elevated around 12 times a year mainly for leisure craft heading upstream to Stockton.

A postcard of Newport Ironworks (Middlesbrough Libraries)

In the shadow of the Tees Newport Bridge is the site of the former Newport Ironworks, established by Sir Bernhard Samuelson in 1864. The works boasted some of the area's largest blast furnaces and supplied iron to Dorman Long's Britannia Works to the east of this site.

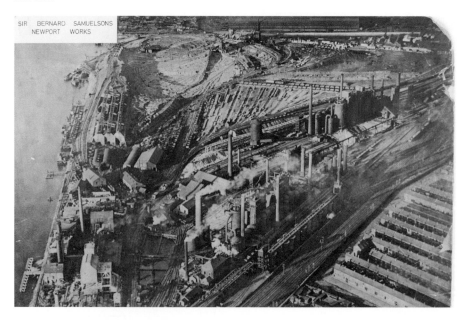

An early twentieth century view of Sir Bernhard Samuelson's Newport Ironworks (Teesside Archives, British Steel Collection)

The interwar years brought cyclical downturns in the iron and steel trade and with Dorman Long increasingly focusing production downstream, Newport Ironworks ceased production in 1930 although the firm had labs at Newport into the post-war years.

Remnants of Newport Ironworks (John Severs)

Severs' photographs allow us to revisit the site and explore remnants of one of Middlesbrough's major ironworks, including the remains of blast furnaces.

"My father worked nearby at Forty Foot Road and I felt an affinity to the area when taking the photographs on the site of Newport Ironworks." - John Severs

The Newport Ironworks site, c.1978 (Teesside Archives)

Having stood empty for decades, in recent years the site has entered a new stage of development through the construction of the Tees Advanced Manufacturing Park (TeesAMP).

Remains of a blast furnace, 2020 (Heritage Unlocked)

The blast furnace remains have been incorporated into a small park as part of the TeesAMP development which has brought manufacturing back to the site over 150 years on from iron production beginning there.

A plan of the former Newport and Britannia works sites, 1983 (Teesside Archives)

A plan of the former Newport and Britannia works sites in 1983 showing the location of a proposed BMX track.

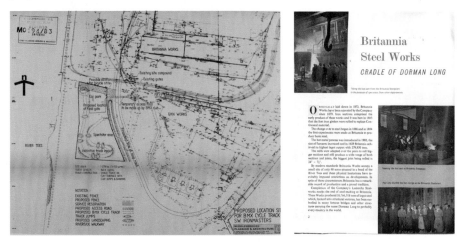

Cradle of Dorman Long, 1954 (Teesside Archives, British Steel Collection)

The Britannia Works, established by Sir Bernhard Samuelson, were acquired by Dorman Long in 1879 and operated into the post-war decades. Here the end of steelmaking at Britannia in 1954 is reported in Dorman Long Illustrated, the company's magazine.

Demolition at Britannia (John Severs)

As part of his interest in capturing disappearing industrial heritage, John Severs captured a number of photographs of the demolition of the Britannia Works.

Britannia Test House, 1960 (Teesside Archives, British Steel Collection)

One of the landmarks that remains from the Britannia Group is the impressive Britannia Test House, which was home to testing equipment on the ground floor used to test components of numerous famous bridges built by Dorman Long, including Sydney Harbour Bridge. This 1960 photograph from Teesside Archives' British Steel Collection shows men at work inside the Test House.

Britannia Works dereliction and the Test House (John Severs)

Now home to Durham Lifting, the Test House continues to be used for proof load testing and testing to destruction a variety of lifting equipment, structures, components, parts and products.

Furness Bridge passes under the Tees Transporter Bridge (Teesside Archives)

Furness Bridge, one of a number of Bridge-class vessels to emerge from Swan Hunter at Haverton Hill, was launched in 1971 as the largest ship built on Teesside. Here Furness Bridge squeezes under the Transporter Bridge and passes along the Tees in the early 1970s.

Launch of the English Bridge, 1972 (John Severs)

John Severs captures the launch of English Bridge, another of the Bridge-class vessels from the former Furness shipyard. Some fourteen years later the vessel, then known as Kowloon Bridge, met an acrimonious end when the ship sunk off the coast of Ireland.

Shaw's Foundry (John Severs)

Another famous name a stone's throw from the Tees was William Shaw's Foundry on Forty Foot Road. Along with the neighbouring British Steel Ayrton Rolling Mills, Shaw's closed in 1985.

"I worked at Shaw's from 1966 to 1971 as an Apprentice Fitter and Turner and worked on a lathe which was 20 foot long. After work, I would call at the Captain Cook and Robin Hood for a pint on the way to catch the no.8 bus home. Happy days and good lads to work with." - David Taylor

William Lane Foundry (Stuart Duffy)

The nearby William Lane Foundry is now the last foundry in Middlesbrough and produces work with a number of projects celebrating the area's heritage.

An AV Dawson heavy haulage vehicle in 1980 (AV Dawson)

AV Dawson's multimodal import and export operations now occupy the former site of Ayrton Rolling Mills, the former Redpath Offshore fabrication sheds and much of the river frontage at Middlesbrough.

The Teessaurus arrives in Middlesbrough (Teesside Archives)

Schoolchildren get a glimpse of the Triceratops outside the Municipal Buildings in 1979 before the dinosaur makes its way to the banks of the River Tees, to be joined the following decade by a number of other dinosaur sculptures.

Teessaurus Park, 2020 (Heritage Unlocked)

In 2020, volunteers helped repaint the dinosaurs at Teessaurus Park which had been graffitied over the years. The sculptures now form part of a colourful, popular visitor attraction.

The Middlesbrough 150 celebrations of 1980 (*The Gazette* & Norman Moorsom)

Against the backdrop of economic turmoil on Teesside with severe job losses in the steel industry and the closure of Middlesbrough Dock, celebrations marking Middlesbrough's 150th birthday took place in 1980.

To Commemorate the 150th Anniversary of the Opening of the
Middlesbrough Branch Railway

and the Shipping of the first Cargo of Coal from
Port Darlington on 27th December, 1830

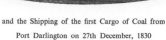

First Day Cover, Middlesbrough 150 celebrations (Heritage Unlocked & Norman Moorsom)

Anniversary events included dinners, exhibitions, lectures and a parade. On 27th December 1980, Jane Hackworth-Young unveiled a plaque marking the 150th anniversary of the inauguration of coal shipping staiths at Port Darlington, now the site of AV Dawson's Port of Middlesbrough facility.

The Tees Transporter Bridge, 1979
(Middlesbrough Libraries)

The 1970s and 1980s proved challenging decades for the Transporter Bridge as debates over the crossing's suitability and frequent closures cast doubt on the landmark's future.

Moneyspinner of White Elephant, 1972 (*The Gazette*)

Between 1976 and 1977, fractures in the rails brought a year-long closure of the Transporter, whilst escalating costs associated with repainting and repairing the structure added fuel to the fire for those looking to close the bridge. Despite the setbacks, the 'Majestic Dinosaur' survived and celebrated its 75th anniversary in October 1986.

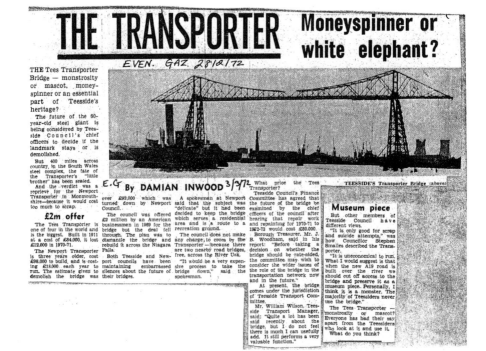

THE TRANSPORTER Moneyspinner or white elephant?

EVEN. GAZ. 28/12/72

E.G By DAMIAN INWOOD 3/3/72

THE Tees Transporter Bridge — monstrosity or mascot, moneyspinner or an essential part of Teesside's heritage?

The future of the 60-year-old steel giant is being considered by Teesside Council's chief officers to decide if the landmark stays or is demolished.

But 400 miles across country, in the South Wales steel complex, the fate of the Transporter's "little brother" has been sealed.

And the verdict was a reprieve for the Newport Transporter in Monmouthshire—because it would cost too much to scrap.

£2m offer

The Tees Transporter is one of four in the world and is the biggest. Built in 1911 at a cost of £84,000, it lost £12,000 in 1970-71.

The Newport Transporter is three years older, cost £98,000 to build, and is costing £18,000 each year to run. The estimate given to demolish the bridge was

over £93,000 which was turned down by Newport Council.

The council was offered £2 million by an American businessmen in 1969 for the bridge but the deal fell through. The plan was to dismantle the bridge and rebuild it across the Niagara Falls.

Both Teesside and Newport councils have been maintaining embarrassed silences about the future of their bridges.

The council decided to keep the bridge which serves a residential area and is a route to a recreation ground.

The council does not make any charge, to cross by the Transporter—because there are two nearby road bridges, free, across the River Usk.

"It would be a very expensive process to take the bridge down," said the spokesman.

A spokesman at Newport said that the subject was "delicate" but it had been decided to keep the bridge which serves a residential area and is a route to a recreation ground.

What price the Tees Transporter?

Teesside Council's Finance Committee has agreed that the future of the bridge be examined by the chief officers of the council after hearing that repair work and repainting for 1970-71 to 1972-73 would cost £80,000.

Borough Treasurer, Mr. J. B. Woodham, said in his report: "Before taking a decision on whether the bridge should be rate-aided, the committee may wish to consider the wider issues of the role of the bridge in the transportation network now and in the future."

At present, the bridge comes under the jurisdiction of Teesside Transport Committee.

Mr. William Wilson, Teesside Transport Manager, said: "Quite a lot has been said recently about the bridge, but I do not feel there is much I can usefully add. It still performs a very valuable function."

Museum piece

But other members of Teesside Council have different views.

"It is only good for scrap and suicide attempts," was how Councillor Stephen Smailes described the Transporter.

"It is uneconomical to run. What I would suggest is that when the new A19 road is built over the river we should cut off access to the bridge and preserve it as a museum piece. Personally, I think it is a monster. The majority of Teessiders never use the bridge."

The Tees Transporter — monstrosity or mascot? Everyone has had their say apart from the Teessiders who look at it and use it. What do you think?

TEESSIDE'S Transporter Bridge (above)

74

Terry's Transporter Trip (*The Gazette*)

The most famous calamity associated with the 'Tranny' occurred in March 1974 when TV personality Terry Scott and his Jaguar took an evening plunge off the Transporter. The Terry and June star believed the bridge to be a conventional crossing and duly crashed into the safety netting below in an embarrassing mishap for both the comedian and the bridge. The incident has since developed a history of its own and become an infamous part of Transporter Bridge folklore!

CARGO FLEET

Customs Row (John Severs)

Built in 1831 to house customs officers, the street was initially known as Queen's Row and later as Customs Row. The terrace of cottages with distinctive octagonal chimneystacks was demolished in the 1980s.

Cargo Fleet Rail Bank (John Severs)

The white painted letters on the bogie bolster wagon reads 'CARGO – RAIL BANK - FLEET'. Railway lines were one of the speciality products of the Cargo Fleet Works.

Demolition of the Cargo Fleet Works (John Severs)

The 1970s and 1980s brought decline for Cargo Fleet and the surrounding communities. The closure of the British Steel Works in the 1980s brought an end to over a century of manufacturing on the site.

Performance details, Cargo Fleet (John Severs)

The performance details of the Cargo Fleet Works are barely visible on the notice board during demolition works.

Cargo Fleet Offices (John Severs)

The Cargo Fleet Offices survived the demolitions and over the past decade have undergone sympathetic renovation. Now home to The Heritage Gallery at Cargo Fleet, the building plays an important role in celebrating the area's iron and steel heritage through the numerous art exhibitions hosted in the gallery spaces.

Cargo Fleet Railway Station (John Severs)

A solitary passenger waits on the platform at Cargo Fleet Railway Station with the steelworks on the horizon.

SOUTH BANK, BRITISH STEEL AND SMITH'S DOCK

The 1970s and 1980s brought challenging times for South Bank with major employers Smith's Dock and British Steel suffering closures and industrial decline. This brought unemployment that has contributed to many moving away from South Bank, businesses closing and housing demolition.

Middlesbrough Road, South Bank, c.1970 (Teesside Archives)

In the 1970s and 1980s, Middlesbrough Road boasted a range of shops, takeaways, pubs and a church.

Bennett's Corner, Normanby Road and Middlesbrough Road (John Severs)

Norman Baum's on Bennett's Corner tries to tempt customers inside with offerings of egg rolls, hamburgers and hotdogs, whilst on Middlesbrough Road fish and chips are on offer at Robinson's.

Napier Street and St Peter's RC
Church (John Severs)

South Bank Market, 1971
(Teesside Archives)

Napier Street was the childhood
home of Wilf Mannion, the South
Bank-born footballer widely
recognised as one of the greatest ever
Middlesbrough and England players.

In Severs' photo the housing has been
demolished and the A66 and a carpark - which
once formed part of South Bank Market - now
occupies the location.

The Alexandra (John Severs)

The Alexandra, known locally as 'The Mucky Pots', was a favourite pub of workers from the
nearby works of British Steel and Smith's Dock

The Zetland, South Bank (John Severs)

Lacking the architectural merits of its Middlesbrough namesake, South Bank's The Zetland nevertheless provokes fond memories amongst former customers.

The Junction (John Severs)

The Junction was a favourite pub of workers at the local industries around South Bank.

"I enjoyed taking photos of the old pubs and communities in South Bank. Pubs were the centres of community and had a lot of history in them and tales to tell. Nobody builds pubs like that anymore." - John Severs

Play Streets, 1972
(Teesside Archives)

A group of children play with a disused, overturned pram on Victoria Street in the early 1970s.

Hampden Street, early 1970s
(Teesside Archives)

An early 1970s view of Hampden Street, the street where the author grew up! The photograph looks eastwards towards Normanby Road.

Smith's Dock, 1986 (Paul Thompson)

These images from photographer Paul Thompson capture Smith's Dock in its later days. The vessel pictured is the 'North Islands', the last ship built at the yard. The ship was launched on 15th October 1986 and the event attracted hundreds of spectators.

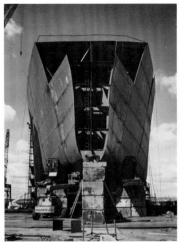

Two Welders at Smith's Dock, 1986 (Paul Thompson)

Two welders on the 'North Islands' stand in front of the ship's bow.

Middlesbrough to Saltburn Railway (John Severs)

The Middlesbrough to Saltburn railway lines and works sidings looking east from Smith's Dock road bridge, with the Clay Lane blast furnaces on the horizon.

Clay Lane Works
(John Severs)

Bell, Blast Furnaces and Gasholder
(John Severs)

The iron and steel industry employed tens of thousands of people from South Bank, Grangetown and the surrounding areas for over a century.

A general view of the Clay Lane blast furnaces and gasholder with a blast furnace bell in the foreground.

Industrial Teesside (John Severs & Paul Sherwood)

These photographs capture industrial Teesside with chemical works, iron and steel production and shipbuilding all featured.

The end of a blast furnace, 1988 (Neil Judson)

Explosives are detonated to mark the end for the redundant Clay Lane blast furnace in 1988.

"I watched the three furnaces being built whilst a pupil at Eston Technical School on Clay Lane. Several decades later, I played a part in designing the control systems for the Redcar furnace. Lots of memories and regrets that more was not done to preserve iron and steel making on the Tees." - David Otterson

Miners secondary picketing at British Steel during the Miners' Strike, Summer 1984. (Paul Thompson)

This picture captures Monkwearmouth miners secondary picketing at British Steel during the Miners' Strike in summer 1984. The Stadium of Light, home of League One Sunderland AFC, now stands on the site of the Monkwearmouth Colliery.

"The picture is a far cry from the Battle of Orgreave which took place around the same time as three Monkwearmouth Colliery miners chat and drink cider with a solitary police officer nearby. I wonder what happened to the miners and the young copper?" - Paul Thompson

LEISURE AND SPORT

Radio Teesside, 1973 (Teesside Archives)

New Year's Eve 1970 saw BBC Radio Teesside launched. This photograph from 1973 shows DJ Dave Eastwood in action at the station.

Bingo at the Empire, early 1980s (Teesside Archives)

Although the Empire is today best known as a nightclub attracting some of the UK's top bands, back in the 1970s and 1980s the former theatre was home to Mecca Bingo.

The ABC Cinema, 1982 (Teesside Archives)

Opened as the Elite in the 1920s, by the 1980s the Linthorpe Road cinema was an EMI owned ABC venue. In this photograph from 1982, Star Trek II: Wrath of Khan tops the bill.

Captain Cook Birthplace Museum (Paul Stephenson)

One of the new additions to Middlesbrough's cultural scene in the 1970s was the Captain Cook Birthplace Museum. Opened in 1978 marking the 250th anniversary of Cook's birth, the Museum is housed in a purpose-built venue close to the granite urn marking the site of Cook's birthplace cottage in Stewart Park.

Middlesbrough Town Hall, 1987 (Middlesbrough Libraries)

Middlesbrough Town Hall played host to a number of leading entertainers and pop stars of the period including David Bowie, The Cure and The Smiths. The billboards in this photograph reveal forthcoming gigs by David Essex, Foster and Allen, The National Youth Brass Band and Victoria Wood.

Gilkes Street Baths (Teesside Archives)

Many Teessiders reminisce about going swimming at Gilkes Street Baths. Once the home pool of Middlesbrough's Olympian swimmer Jack Hatfield, the baths were demolished in the 1990s and Captain Cook Square now stands on the site.

Charlton's Champions, 1974 (Middlesbrough FC) and the Ayresome Park floodlights visible from one of the alleys near the stadium (John Severs)

The 1970s brought a renaissance under the stewardship of 'Big Jack' Charlton, including promotion to the top-flight in 1974. The decade brought an Anglo-Scottish Cup success, a League Cup semi-final appearance and a number of FA Cup quarter-final appearances as Boro threatened to bring elusive major silverware back to Teesside.

One of the epicentres of sporting life of 1970s and 1980s Middlesbrough was Ayresome Park, the home of Middlesbrough Football Club. The two decades proved to be amongst the most dramatic in Boro's history with the club securing several promotions, suffering several relegations and surviving near extinction.

Big John Hickton, 1977
(Middlesbrough FC)

The 1970s also saw some of
Boro's greatest players turn
out for the club at Ayresome
Park, including goalscoring
hero John Hickton, midfield
maestro Graeme Souness and
local star Willie Maddren.

Night to Remember, 1983
(Middlesbrough Libraries & *The Gazette*)

The 1980s saw a downturn in
fortunes with relegation from the
top-flight, financial turmoil that
resulted in the sale of star
players, eventual relegation to
the third-tier and the club on the
brink of bankruptcy. One of the
few highlights of the early 1980s
was the Wilf Mannion and
George Hardwick testimonial
match at Ayresome Park in May
1983.

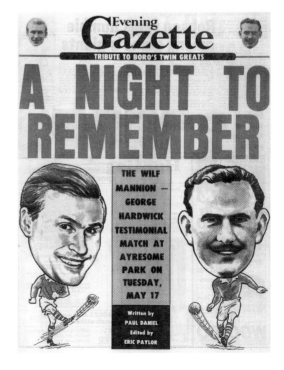

Boro are saved as the padlock comes off the gates at Ayresome Park (Middlesbrough FC)

Boro were saved at the eleventh hour in 1986 by a consortium led by Steve Gibson. Bruce Rioch's 'Class of '86' included many players who had come from the ranks at Ayresome Park and went on to secure back-to-back promotions to bring top-flight football back to Teesside.

The Ayresome Crowd, 1988 (Tom Collins)

Photographer Tom Collins captures a packed Holgate End during Bradford City's visit to Ayresome Park in February 1988.

Ripley Hat Trick Sparks Spree (*Evening Gazette* & Middlesbrough Libraries)

Boro produced a number of fantastic players during that period including future England internationals Colin Cooper, Gary Pallister and Stuart Ripley.

"I attended my first Boro match at the age of four on 2nd April 1988 at Ayresome Park with Sheffield United the opposition. My Dad said he couldn't take me in the Holgate as it was too cold and couldn't get in the Clive Road End so we instead ended up watching the match from the 'Chicken Run'. I can't remember the match although I wish I could as we won 6-0!" - Tosh Warwick

Boro celebrate promotion, 1988 (Middlesbrough FC)

Middlesbrough players celebrate promotion to the top flight at Stamford Bridge in 1988. A 2-1 play-off aggregate win over Chelsea secured back-to-back promotions for Bruce Rioch's men.

Boro v Manchester United matchday programme, 1989 (Middlesbrough FC)

Boro's top-flight campaign ultimately brought the disappointment of relegation despite some impressive results, including a 1-0 win over Manchester United in January 1989.

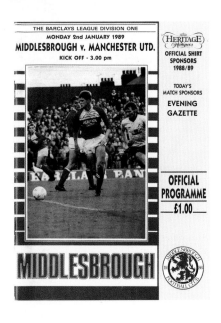

Normanby Road Ground, c.1970 (John Wakelin)

South Bank narrowly missed out on Northern League Cup glory in the 1980s and at their highpoint attracted thousands of supporters at the Normanby Road Ground.

Normanby Road with the football stadium on the right, 1970s (Eric Taylor)

South Bank once possessed one of the finest teams in the region and produced a number of future Middlesbrough and England stars.

A speedway meeting at Cleveland Park in the 1980s (Paul Stephenson)

Greyhound racing and speedway at Cleveland Park Stadium was a popular sporting attraction in the 1970s and 1980s.

A programme from the Middlesbrough v Milton Keynes meeting at Cleveland Park, 1986 (Paul Stephenson)

An arson attack at Cleveland Park in 1985 devastated the main stand. Despite this setback, greyhound racing and speedway continued at Cleveland Park into the mid-1990s when the site was sold and the stadium demolished.

Opening of Tennis World, 1986 (Teesside Archives)

British tennis ace Roger Taylor MBE officially opened the new Tennis World Indoor Centre at Marton Road in December 1986 and found time to exhibit his serve for guests at the event.

Boycott in the Boro, 1971 (*The Gazette*)

Acklam Park served as one of Yorkshire Cricket Club's home venues from the 1950s until the 1990s and a number of the game's top players turned out in first-class matches at Middlesbrough. Here newly appointed Yorkshire captain Geoffrey Boycott leads his team out for the first time for their match with Warwickshire at Acklam Park in May 1971.